NEW ARTS

Nisha Bhakoo is based in Angus, Scotland. She has had three poetry collections published and edited the *Contemporary Gothic Verse Anthology* published by The Emma Press. She has a PhD in Creative Writing from the University of Dundee and has also taught literature-based modules at the University of Dundee, University of Potsdam, and Humboldt University, as well as at The Poetry School. She has recently been awarded funding for her writing by Creative Scotland and Society of Authors.

Also by Nisha Bhakoo

Spectral Forest   (The Onslaught Press, 2020)

Contemporary Gothic Verse [editor]   (The Emma Press, 2019)

Black & White Dream   (Broken Sleep Books, 2018)

You Found a Beating Heart   (The Onslaught Press, 2016)

Contents

Part One: The Art of Dying

Part Two: Dark Arts

ISBN: 978-1-917617-31-4

Cover designed by Aaron Kent

Edited and Typeset by Aaron Kent

Broken Sleep Books Ltd
PO BOX 102
Llandysul
SA44 9BG

For Mum and Dad

New Arts

Nisha Bhakoo

Broken Sleep Books

Part One:
The Art of Dying

Part One

The Art of Dying

TANGERINE

A tangerine in a pigeon-hole. Left by your ghost? I go through the motions in my baggy dress, mascara and lip-gloss. Do I pass as a good employee? I have taken the tough fruit of grief. I crumble into a crumpled tissue in the toilet cubicle at lunch. Peel the skin of rot ten citrus back. My soul has sepsis. Council tax to pay.

GUMMIES

There are vases and cards pricked up on every surface. People in their neatest handwriting have written *sorry for your loss*. I cannot comfort you, nor do I want to. I give you a palmful of CBD gummies and say *chew*. We pin all of our hopes on the unknowns of night – on dreams, apparitions, ectoplasm – not God.

STORIES IN THE MOSS

Soon – stories in the moss. The past lies under ice. Letting the people sleep – almost. Secrets in glib objects. The bathtub is frosty. The woman hibernates. Her unconscious – awake – in the stonework. I suddenly smell spring. All the buried secrets will bloom into being overnight. The ice will take off suddenly like a plane.

CARNIVOROUS GHOSTS

Beware – while you nibble on your iceberg lettuce, the dead are eating you from the inside. Carnivorous ghosts. Chewing the root of your heart. Sucking on your jawbone like it is liquorice root. The dead engulf your memories then spit them out when you are too drunk on vodka, their names surface like ingrowing hairs.

LACK

Lives soaked in brine and fresh desire. We count pocket cents on the way to *Imrans*. Cyanide words fuelled by scarcity and splitting bills. The whoosh of the underpass reminds us we are outside, so we should act like it. Alone in the shop. We wait on our falafels, jittery at a joint excess of lack. Mouths full of saliva.

THERAPIST

Those who let too many powders slip through the cracks of floorboards are estranged from vitality. Disembodied. My constant summer sniffle is in fact raw grief. Carving a smile on to mouth instead of roast chicken on Sundays when I set out to see my therapist. I imagine her outside of work. Preheating her huge oven.

SNOW DAY

We did not anticipate the snow breaking through the ceiling. Turning the carpet white with shock. Building a snowman – abracadabra! In the toilet bowl. Icing stiff the handles of doors so we remain like statues. There is a creeping loneliness that comes in with snow like Fridays spent in high-street betting shops.

TRINKETS

She left us nothing except a tiny box of trinkets. Before she passed, she said, keep it safe. A whole life in a silver box for such a personality. Out of sight. Too small to sum her up. In the coffin, she looked like a porcelain doll. Hair pinned back with metal hairpins. She never combed her fine hair. Body silky as a tofu tongue.

THE KIEZ

Stodge of grey leaves at the communal entrance. Swept away by *Hausmeister* in a slick move. Craving grungy freedom, a glimmer of spit and fine dirt that brought you here. Soggy autumn wastes. Stale beer on jeans. The Kiez is being sanitized. Make Berlin shit again. Cleanliness is godliness. We don't believe in God.

BAD FUCK

January, I put my legs in between a sheet of ice. Celibate but melting. I took a bite of February, then spat it up. A blend of March voices. Under ribbons, I came. Pornographic. What is it about April? The nights pull hair, grab at my wrists. May was sour under the eyes. Enough of magazines, make-up tips. Baby, I am natural.

But June, put the days between the knife and sliced right through them. Therapeutic. Dangerous. I wouldn't say July was enjoyable, but it needed to be worked through. It was constant stops and starts in August. Then in my birth month of September, I finally realized that the lid did not fit the jar perfectly and moved on – October was not easy, but freedom never is. November, still full of tacky Halloween goodies, I was yawning until December.

Listen – listen – it turns again. Listen – round and round. And then comes the 31st – we ask the wheel to turn gently. But it never does. It jerks, it stagnates, it rolls over fat globs of glass. A nasty, bad fuck, you see through to the very end.

IMPOSSIBLE STORY

The mouth cannot lose the tongue,
but it can be silenced by fear.
Chewing on toffees.
Censoring verbs.
Writing an impossible story.

I cannot create from clay
when the creation is stuffed
into a dark cupboard.

I go out to capture a flash of sun,
it is raining cats and rats.
I touch my crocodile skin,
starved of nutrients and care.

They say, *the Holy Spirit lives within*.
I try to keep my heartrate down
to make it a comfortable home.

Storm-licked in our apartments.
We should all take to the streets.

HUMBOLDTHAIN

Midnight comes early in this city.

Make-up wipes strewn in the bin.

Ready for another insect-light sleep.

Counting between days and the delicious

hailstorms of Humboldthain.

The internal-gymnastics –

racing thoughts of unbelonging.

Avoiding the cracks in the pavement.

This city never learns its lesson,

and neither do I.

I have returned too many times to

remember its gut-punch.

Part Two:
Dark Arts

NEW ARTS

We hover above car bonnets.
Teleportation, levitation.
Trampling the rows of root vegetables
as we land on two solid feet.

Your mouth is a cauldron.

We take steps beyond existence into
the long corridor of discovery.
Wiping down dusty videotapes:
tiny truths, tiny lies.

The next day, during migraine
the vibrations of the body
are felt intensely.
Every routine peeled away

like a lunch-time banana.
The kitchen: the bone of the house –
sitting there for hours,
playing out yesterday's events.
Language slipping inwards
from an easy tongue.

Enamoured by these new arts.

COCOON

Snug as a mushroom.

      The pulse pleads.

          Inside the egg.

              Safe as Spring.

                    Cocoon of boredom.

                        Fibers too flimsy to strangle!

                        Even a little one.

She, not chanterelle.

She, too safe to move – until

the summer she hatched.

Alive, shimmering.

Sticky shell got everywhere.

                  Or was it a life enclosed?

                        In-edible.

MOONWORT

The meat of your language
is pale, unappetizing.

> The Baobhan Sith
> will not even take its blood.

Let in the unknown.
The ultimate surprise –

> your capacity for love.
> When you hoard:

silvery full moons in your pocket
to unlock dark, *oriental* doors.

SHED

Grass stains on jeans and jackets / They sit for hours, clams of
the land / Girling into meatless fists / Marbles of ideas and innovation
swallowed by school and sleep / Family sandstorms / disorienting
the soundest minds /At sixteen the snakes will shed their skin /
They will strike / Women will strike /

CHEWING OVER

Gathering stichwort to enter the fairy realms.
It is hard to stay here in this city.
Frostbite creeping into the heart.
Cream in a saucer, a hip flask of whisky.
Soon to be drunk by the fairies.
Abandoned novels and layers of bright fabric
cannot mark me out from other humans.

The discomfort of sharing similar bones
must be sat with tonight. The fairies are busy.
Toes discover dust at the foot of the sofa.
Chewing over – creating space for others,
all of them. My bones how they ache.
There is no enemy, no strange land.
We share similar desires, similar teeth.

NORTH SEA ANGELS

North Sea angels capture the eyes
of those who visit alone.

The waves hold hands,
perform circus acts.

Spinning into shimmering wheels,
thrusting wet fists close to the shore.

When you have had quite enough,
they take a bow.

Another bow
to wrap around your dreams.

SIGNATURE

The game is organized in a zig-zag of vitality and illness.

Authorised. The percentage of cold evenings

and those of heat cracking the palms.

The signature is our choice. Imprint into being.

Roots reaching out to caress each other under the soil.

Odd little intervals of pink glowing buds.

The swimming of growing intimacies.

But then – counting noiseless tears until sunrise.

Breakups, death of loved-ones, famine,

wars, injustice galore, the trauma of breath.

Placing periwinkle on to the ground before the moon.

Surrendering to the status of living in a topsy-turvy world.

LEVITATE

Mid-sentence, hand freezes.
Refuses to perform a circus act,
to braid children's hair all night.

To remove a thick film of grease from the dishes
each morning, each afternoon, each night.
The bracelets of expectation are taken off,

shimmering soles levitate from a beige carpet.
Young red branches reach out to you.
Thrill ripples through the tongue.

Clouds clear to bestow a gift.
Our new language is gigantic.
Our new language writes over:

the language of capitalism.

MONDAY

Every Monday she wears lace gloves.

Every Monday she hides the white buds of teeth

when she asks me for rent, rent, rent, rent, rent, rent, rent, rent, rent, rent, rent, rent, rent, rent, rent, rent rent, rent, rent, rent, rent, rent, rent, rent, rent, rent, rent, rent, rent, rent rent, rent, rent, rent, rent rent, rent.

No slither of emotion.

Every Monday, her eyes: white as eggs.

Every Monday it is crisis o'clock.

CYCLE

The sun sings
a splitting November song
of peace and war.

The day's cycle is not complete.
Outside, the children fight over
a tatty bicycle.

They push each other as I cut
down spiky branches
from the mouths of strangers.

Feet pass by my stepladder
into the fading credits of the film.
The sky darkens,

the cycle is on its way
to completion,
to starting all over again – again –

ACKNOWLEDGEMENTS

'Shed' was first published in Issue 81 - The Interpreter's House.

Thanks to Society of Authors and Creative Scotland for supporting my writing, and a big shout out to Aaron Kent and the wonderful team at Broken Sleep Books for continuing to support my poetry.

LAY OUT YOUR UNREST

www.ingramcontent.com/pod-product-compliance
Lightning Source LLC
LaVergne TN
LVHW041328080426
835513LV00008B/640